WILLIAM SANCHES

50 Questions about the Law of attraction FOR BEGINNERS

50 questions about the law of attraction for beginners
Copyright © 2021 by William Sanches

All rights reserved: Citadel Editorial SA

The contents of this book are the sole responsibility of the author and do not necessarily reflect the views of the publisher.

ISBN 978-1-64095-626-1
eBook ISBN 978-1-64095-627-8
1 2025

Editorial production and distribution:

contato@citadel.com.br
www.citadel.com.br

Distributed in English language by:
SOUND WISDOM
P.O. Box 310 • Shippensburg, PA 17257-0310 • 717-530-2122
info@soundwisdom.com

WILLIAM SANCHES

50 Questions about the Law of attraction FOR BEGINNERS

Preface

Everything good and bad in your life is the result of the Law of Attraction.

Every event, feeling, person or situation, however mundane and insignificant they may seem, has an important purpose in your evolutionary journey, and the Law of Attraction is present in each of them.

The Law of Attraction is a universal algorithm, installed on our planet so that we can bring situations, people and events together at all times that can provide us with learning and evolution.

Do you think or do they think for you?

Are you who you really want to be?

What paradigms are guiding you?

These questions are provocations for us to experience the freedom of being the conscious creators of our reality!

We are all creators of our reality. Because everything we experience in the present is the result of our past choices, and what we need is to create reality in a more planned and conscious way, and this is possible when we get in touch with the rules of this algorithm called the Law of Attraction.

Most of us human beings are encouraged to buy into ready-made, processed, diluted ideas. Therefore, we are encouraged not to think and so we create mistaken beliefs that form our paradigm, which is a set of feelings, thoughts, emotions and beliefs (often limiting) that prevent us from fully experiencing our potential and living in absolute freedom.

Think about it: how many times have you wanted to do certain things, but stopped doing them because it didn't seem right in society's eyes? How many times have you repressed your desires? All of this is the result of the belief system that governs us and prevents us from being absolutely free and happy.

To break free, you need to break patterns and invest in your self-knowledge!

In this excellent book, our friend William Sanches demonstrates the secrets of the Law of Attraction in a light and very practical way, and how you can apply it to your life in a practical and fun way, achieving those goals, desires and conquests that have been postponed, dusty and often forgotten inside you.

Everything you think and feel, the universe gives back to you in the same proportion and harmony!

Try to imagine yourself as a big magnet, and start nourishing your soul only with high-vibration thoughts and feelings. And if I had to leave you with just one piece of advice about the Law of Attraction, it would be: exercise true gratitude, the kind that comes from the heart, and admire other people's success. And I say this because, with this tip, you'll already be acting in the direction of your dreams!

Being grateful directs your focus to what has already been achieved, and the universe understands that you want to achieve more!

When we focus on what we don't yet have, the focus is directed towards scarcity, and the universe understands that you want more scarcity...

It sounds cliché and too simple, but if you try it out, you'll be able to prove the Law of Attraction in practice.

Furthermore, admiring other people's success and celebrating their achievements as if they were our own increases our potential for attraction, because our mind doesn't differentiate between fiction and reality. So if I'm celebrating someone else's success, I'm attracting success for myself, because for the mind, success is success. Whether this success is mine or someone else's makes no difference to the attraction.

The Law of Attraction works for everyone, regardless of gender, age, profession or creed, because it is inherent in the human soul.

We're all subject to it and there's no escaping it: either you discover its subtleties and secrets to transform your life forever, or you continue to be subject to the consequences of the "herd effect", feeling powerless, underutilized, one more in a crowd of people dissatisfied with the economy, the government or their work; who spend their lives complaining and talking about it, and end up not achieving their dreams and goals.

How about getting out of the mainstream and becoming someone who, like a drone, can fly overhead and see everything from above, anticipating trends and finding the best solutions? How about having a more peaceful and balanced life, without so many energy swings, so many ups and downs, and living happier and with more joy throughout the week, at all times, and not just on weekends and vacations?

This is our invitation for you to dive into this work and transform your life forever, achieving prosperity, abundance, happiness, personal power, self-esteem, bliss and fulfillment.

You already know how to attract everything you want, but you've just disconnected from this function!

By reading this book to the end and immersing yourself in what William proposes, you will once again be able to create the life of your dreams. And believe me, it is possible!

Shall we go together?

Love, Patrícia Cândido.

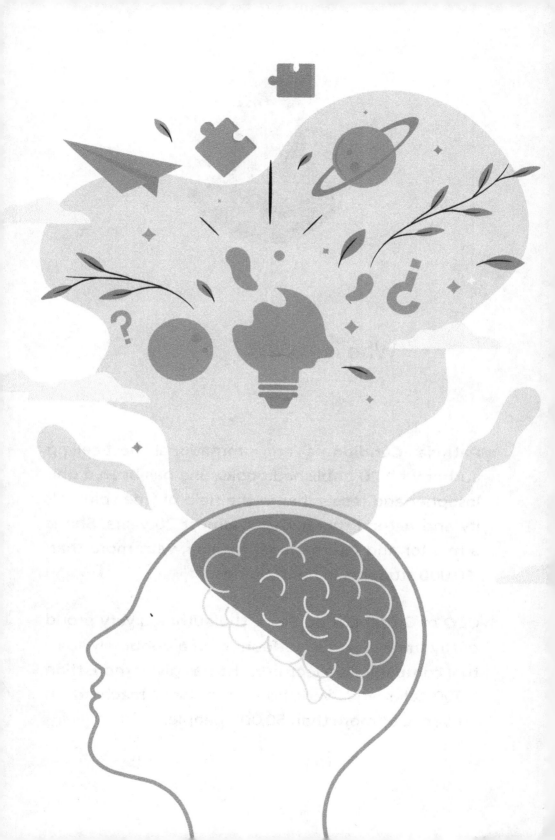

Who is Patrícia Cândido?

Patrícia Cândido is an international best-selling author with 20 published books. She has been a philosopher and researcher in the field of free spirituality and natural therapies for almost 20 years. She is a mentor and international speaker, with more than 150,000 students in her trainings.

CEO of Grupo Luz da Serra, the author is very proud to say that she is the co-founder of a genuinely spiritual company. As a lecturer, she has given more than 2,000 talks and workshops in person, reaching an audience of more than 50,000 people.

Featured on the YouTube channel Luz da Serra, which has more than 2 million followers, she addresses issues of well-being and spirituality, which transform the lives of thousands of people every day.

Patrícia is the World Ambassador for Phytoenergetics and is recognized by the national and international press. She has collaborated with magazines such as Negócios, Exame, Bons Fluídos, Glamour and Estadão, as well as taking part in various TV programs on Band and TV Gazeta.

Introduction

For a long time, one question plagued me: why do some people have everything, and easily, while others take their time and often don't get what they want?

There must have been something different about these people. After all, they all had the same conditions, lived in the same country and, some of them, even had the same family.

Why did some go so far and others always skate?

For years I had been bothered by my situation of scarcity and, like a prospector who goes into deep, dark caves and digs through the hard rock in search of diamonds, I looked for how successful people thought, spoke, felt, behaved...

I've always been passionate about questions of the soul, feelings and the mind.

No wonder I became a good therapist.

I've read and studied everything, watched videos, read books and lost count of how many lectures and courses I've taken in this area.

I can't tell you when I first came into contact with the expression "Law of Attraction", but I do know that it was when all the loose pieces I had came together, like in an old jigsaw puzzle, to make sense of everything!

I've always been very curious, which motivated me to learn more about the Law of Attraction and its mysteries.

I believed in better days and I knew that abundance was for me, but I didn't know how to actually get there and stay there.

So I decided to delve into quantum physics, neuroscience and this so-called Law of Attraction, which had a real boom in 2006 with the release of the documentary and book "THE SECRET" by Rhonda Byrne.

This was a watershed book that made the Law of Attraction known. But not in depth!

That's right: at the same time as this powerful law has generated immense marketing, spreading it all over the world, for many people it has created the opposite effect: people have started to think that only the power of thought can change our reality and that if we spend hours thinking positively, meditating and saying "gratitude", things will start to happen and wishes will come true magically!

That's not all.

The Law of Attraction is an incredible cog in the wheel.

It doesn't work on its own. It is closely linked to other universal laws, such as the law of free will, action and reaction, vibration, reciprocity, rhythm...

It is a piece that, if understood and put into practice in the right way, transforms lives, YES!

The secret is just knowing how to use it correctly and not being too lazy to learn.

It was not only for this reason that I decided to write this quick and didactic guide, but I also realized the need that people have been presenting to co-create a healthier and more harmonious reality, and I also felt that we are ready to revive this subject of quantum physics and the Law of Attraction, only this time, in a simple way and with the great secret actually revealed!

This guide is for those people who want to start learning this universal law and transform their lives in a positive way and manifest their desires based on years of study, in which I was the scientist, the experiment and the result.

Today, I live a successful life. Everything I will teach you in this book has been applied in my life and in the lives of many people who have transformed their realities of difficulty, pre-occupation and pain into a life of ease, creativity and virtue through my courses and books.

I compare each question to a step. A great ladder starts with the first rung. Step by step, stage by stage. Do the same.

Study, understand, apply.

It will certainly be worth every step.

— William Sanches

SUMÁRIO

22
QUESTION 1
What is the Law of Attraction?

24
QUESTION 2
What can you attract with the Law of Attraction?

28
QUESTION 3
How to work with and put into practice the Law of Attraction?

30
QUESTION 4
What steps can lead to mistakes in the Law of Attraction?

32
QUESTION 5
Is the Law of Attraction literally attracting things into our lives?

34
QUESTION 6
I can want several things at the same time or I need to focus on something specific

36
QUESTION 7
Can I use the Law of Attraction to drive away people who aren't good for me?

38
QUESTION 8
Can negative thinking affect the Law of Attraction?

40
QUESTION 9
If everyone started using the Law of Attraction, using it as a catalog, wouldn't there be a shortage of resources in the universe?

44
QUESTION 10
What can I do to start using the Law of Attraction today?

52
QUESTION 11
Why can't I use the Law of Attraction to win the lottery?

56
QUESTION 12
I have a legal case and I used the Law of Attraction, but I couldn't win. What did I do wrong?

58
QUESTION 13
For the Law of Attraction to work, do you have to ask, feel and let go?

62
QUESTION 14
Can I use the Law of Attraction to attract a specific person?

64
QUESTION 15
How do I change my energy signature?

68
QUESTION 16
Why doesn't the Law of Attraction work for me?

72
QUESTION 17
I don't believe in the Law of Attraction. How can I change that?

76
QUESTION 18
"Thoughts are things." What do you mean, William? I didn't understand that!

80
QUESTION 19
Can you lose weight with the Law of Attraction?

86
QUESTION 20
How can blocking feelings influence the Law of Attraction in someone's life?

90
QUESTION 21
How long does it take to see the results of the Law of Attraction?

94
QUESTION 22
You say that our thoughts become feelings and vibrations. Is that the Law of Attraction?

98
QUESTION 23
How does it work when we think something and the exact opposite happens?

102
QUESTION 24
How do we find out which blockages are getting in the way?

106
QUESTION 25
Is discouragement a block to the Law of Attraction?

112
QUESTION 26
Can I use the Law of Attraction to win the lottery?

116
QUESTION 27
When the fear is so great that you can't co-create anything... What do you do?

120
QUESTION 28
When you say that the Law of Attraction can be accelerated, does that mean that this acceleration is natural, as long as I change my vibration pattern?

122
QUESTION 29
Does being a "cowhand" affect the Law of Attraction in my life?

126
QUESTION 30
Can we change our unconscious to attract better things faster?

128
QUESTION 31
Can I attract things to other people using the Law of Attraction?

130
QUESTION 32
How can we control thoughts that automatically come into our minds?

132
QUESTION 33
Is there a step-by-step process for applying the Law of Attraction in my daily life, or is it a study that takes effect over time?

134
QUESTION 34
They say you can use the Law of Attraction to make someone else think of you. Is this true?

136
QUESTION 35
When we're vibrating in something good and suddenly negative thoughts come up that we've been carrying around all our lives and that "erase" that good vibration that was there before, is there any way to get me back to the good vibration?

138
QUESTION 36
How can I vibrate that I deserve a job if I've been unemployed for months?

142
QUESTION 37
William, I'm on disability pension and I have a chronic illness. I need a job that won't jeopardize my pension. I have a master's degree in literature and a lot of studies.

144
QUESTION 38
When I stop feeling rejected by a certain situation, does that mean that my mind has been unblocked?

146
QUESTION 39
How do I deal with the feeling of always being "sucked in" by someone negative around me? How do I keep my energy up?

148
QUESTION 40
How do I know if I'm practicing the Law of Attraction correctly?

150
QUESTION 41
Does the Law of Attraction interfere with our destiny?

152
QUESTION 42
My husband is extremely negative and that saddens me because I love him. How do I deal with this situation?

156
QUESTION 43
Is it wrong to co-create the "dream house" instead of co-create the renovation of your current home?

158
QUESTION 44
Does the Law of Attraction have anything to do with religion?

160
QUESTION 45
Does the Law of Attraction need to be activated to work?

162
QUESTION 46
Is it possible to use the Law of Attraction to treat physical and emotional pain?

166
QUESTION 47
Is the Law of Attraction a form of prayer?

170
QUESTION 48
Is there a method to make the Law of Attraction work faster?

174
QUESTION 49
My friend doesn't believe in the Law of Attraction, she thinks it's all nonsense. How can this influence me?

176
QUESTION 50
Now that I've studied everything about the Law of Attraction, can I stop studying and the Law will take care of everything?

50 questions about the

Law of Attraction

"Like all the laws of nature, this law is absolutely perfect. You create your life. You reap what you sow! Your thoughts are the seeds, and your harvest will depend on the kind of seeds you plant."

— Rhonda Byrne

1 What is the Law of Attraction?

It's a **natural law of the universe,** which governs us in the world, just like the law of gravity, just like the law of free will, for example.

Everything you think, feel and vibrate, you are automatically, through the power of your thoughts, attracting into your life, your reality.

The **Law of Attraction** attracts to us what we think about, whether consciously or unconsciously.

The **Law of Attraction** is always at work, whether you believe in it or not.

You attract what you are!

The Universe gives you more of the same, no matter where you live or how old you are. You and I work with an incredible power: attraction.

"It's a pleasure and a joy to plant new seeds, because I know that they will become my new experiences.

Now, I choose to make my life light, easy and joyful.

With ease and freedom, I let go of the old and happily welcome the new."

2 What can you attract with the Law of Attraction?

Watch out! Each of your thoughts is a real thing when we talk about attraction.

In other words, you can do anything! No matter what you have in mind, you can bring it to yourself. You can do anything, but not everything is good for you.

Let's imagine something really crazy to use as an example: I want to take a trip to the moon. So ask yourself:

"Is that within my reach now?"

I'm not telling you to limit your dream, but you have to keep your feet on the ground. Ask yourself:

> "**How many years will I have to study** to get into NASA?
>
> **At what age do they usually** send people to the moon?
>
> **How much time do I need to** spend in my life **to get to the moon?**"

Do you understand?

You need to have a dream, a desire, a measurable, tangible attraction so that it can come into your life. Otherwise, you'll just be wasting your time, skating along, not believing in the Law of Attraction.

"I love and approve of myself. In this way, I am able to create an abundant life.

I recognize in myself all the power of the universe.

Everything I desire is within my being."

3 How to work with and put into practice the Law of Attraction?

We are working with the **Law of Attraction** all the time. So when we think something, we automatically emit an energy or vibrational frequency onto the planet. You don't need to "activate" anything! It, like every natural law of the universe, is already active.

Imagine this: when you turn on the radio to listen to rock or country music, you're tuning into a radio frequency that will bring you an answer.

Remember that every time we think, we emanate electromagnetic waves, attracting to us everything we want.

You don't have to "put it into practice", because it's working all the time. You have to learn how it works more quickly and with positive results.

It's interesting to know that we can create and control our external reality through the powerful knowledge of the Law of Attraction.

"I leave my mind free of boycotting thoughts so that the universe can connect me with the best.

I trust the universe and its laws."

4 Which steps can lead to mistakes in the Law of Attraction?

We don't consider mistakes in the **Law of Attraction**, but we can attract things that aren't so clear, for example:

"I really want a good boyfriend". But what would a "good boyfriend" be for you?

An honest **man?**

A working **man?**

Is a good boyfriend a good man in bed**?**

Realize that, for each person, "good" can mean different things. So the clearer you are about your goal, the fewer mistakes you'll make.

"I have very clear objectives and goals.

The universe understands well what I want and manifests it according to my clarity."

5 Is the Law of Attraction literally attracting things into our lives?

If, when you wake up, you think: "I'm going to be late for the meeting and hit traffic", you are emanating an energy, sending an electromagnetic frequency out into the universe and instantly attracting things to yourself that will, in fact, create that reality. You will be delayed more and more. You have issued an order.

We have to have a very clear idea in our minds: we are a human magnet, attracting everything we think, feel and vibrate. You are the most powerful magnet in the universe right now. We have a very strong magnetic power within us. This power is radiated by our predominant thoughts.

We are, AT ALL TIMES, attracting things, people and situations, but the attraction and manifestation of desire begins with our thoughts. Therefore, what we think and, above all, what we feel, is what will be attracted to our current reality.

"I am a human magnet, attracting all prosperity, wealth and opportunities into my life."

6 Can I want several things at the same time or do I need to focus on something specific?

We can desire several things at once, yes. But where we focus, we amplify the energy.

For example: you may want to get your driver's license, go on a trip abroad, get your passport, become a millionaire, have your own house on the beach or lose weight, but you're emanating a little bit of energy for each thing. If you focus directly and put all your energy towards one desire, you have a better chance of doing it faster and succeeding.

It's working on distributing your focus in an intelligent and productive way!

My tip is to focus on a goal and create targets.

At this point, it's absolutely fine to have secondary goals on the way to your objective, as long as you never lose focus on achieving it.

"My ideas are incredible and I have the creative energy to bring them to life.

My thoughts of prosperity create my prosperous world."

7 Can I use the Law of Attraction to drive away people who are not good for me?

Yes.

Think of those people being happy away from you, traveling far away. You don't have to wish them harm simply because you don't want them around anymore. Life is made up of cycles and sometimes that friendship, that relationship, that marriage, is over. It's smart to move on and detach.

The opposite is also true. Have you ever been thinking a lot about someone, picked up your cell phone and got a message from them? You sent electromagnetic waves to them and connected with their energy.

If you don't want to connect with someone anymore, don't think about them. Always think of them going away from you, and put another energy in place of the energy they had inside you. Stop occupying your mind with that person. Change your focus and your energy will also change and, consequently, your power of attraction.

"I'm free to be myself and I give others the freedom to be who they are.

I'm surrounded by good people who influence me positively in my life."

8 Can negative thinking affect the Law of Attraction?

Every thought is creating your reality.

It's not that it "affects" the Law of Attraction. Remember that it is working all the time.

What happens is this: if we think negative thoughts, then negative reality comes to us, because it has become the predominant thought.

The Law of Attraction is not a button that you turn on and off. It is working all the time, in its entirety, even when we sleep or wake up. There's no turning it on and off. So if I'm thinking negatively, I'm building a negative reality for myself. And that's a real problem: having an extremely negative mental pattern!

Positive thinking is training!

"My mind is prosperous and always works forward.

I can turn any unproductive thought into profitable ideas, any negativity into positivity.

My mind is getting better every day!"

9 If everyone started using the Law of Attraction, and using it as a catalog, wouldn't there be a shortage of resources in the universe?

No!

The universe has everything we need and, what's more, each person has a different type of desire.

Not everyone wants a white car. There are people who like black or silver cars. So the universe is a big catalog and, when we open this catalog of desires, we choose the life we want to have.

This question shows that the person who asked it vibrates more in scarcity. Hence this fear of lack.

The universe is abundant, nothing will be lacking.

And when it's lacking, it's because of evil or the reality of scarcity generated by the person.

Always remember that we are the ones building our own reality.

We are exactly where we put ourselves and, if we worry, thinking that there will be a lack of resources in the universe because everyone knows the Law of Attraction, we are in the energy of scarcity, thinking about lack, with the feeling of fear, vibrating in scarcity and, possibly, only this kind of thing will happen in our lives.

Change that low frequency, your question shows your pattern of lack and selfishness.

Your worries prevent you from being creative, rich and abundant!

Rethink your patterns and find out where this fear of lacking things comes from.

"Everything I want is already available in the universe, which is abundant and unlimited!

I deserve wealth and prosperity!"

10. What can I do to start using the Law of Attraction today?

You are already using the Law of Attraction, asleep and awake.

> **It rules you at all times. So let's change the question:**
>
> How can I now be clear about my desires, so that the Law of Attraction can help me get them fulfilled much faster?

It's gotten better, hasn't it?

If you don't have clarity, it's just a vague desire, a crazy idea that has crossed your mind, a floating dream.

So how do we know we're there?

If we're at point A and we're going to point B, there's a route to get there. So we need to move.

Faith generates action and action generates miracles. We can call your fulfillment a miracle, that desire you have in your life! You have to know where you are now and where you want to go.

I'm going to help you very quickly. Take a look at the questions I've prepared for you.

Use them at any time, throughout your time of co-creating a new reality. These questions clarify paths.

Point A

Where are you now? Where do you live? What do you do for a living? What is your current situation?

_____

_____

_____

_____

_____

_____

_____

_____

_____

Point B

What is my main objective? What are the details? When do I want to achieve it?

Traject

What resources do I need now? How can I best prepare for my goal? Are there people or situations that can help me? If it's up to me, am I doing my best?

_____
_____
_____
_____
_____
_____
_____
_____
_____
_____

Traject

Do I know people who have achieved this goal? I know I have my own way, but how did they do it? Can this help me clarify my path?

"I'm creative, intelligent and I know exactly where I want to go and how I'm going to get there!"

11 Why can't I use the Law of Attraction to win the lottery?

When we set ourselves the goal of winning a prize, we are taking away from ourselves any value, ability or capacity to achieve a result. And it will be in this inability and incapacity that we will vibrate and, obviously, not connect to any prize. On the contrary!

I often say that luck is the combination of opportunity and preparation.

The opportunity to play is there and it's the same for everyone. But what about preparation?

At this point, you're probably thinking:

> "But William, do you need preparation to be rich?"

Yes, it takes preparation to be rich!

Think of how many lottery winners have lost everything or even become poorer than before they won.

What happened to these people is that they weren't prepared for that fortune: they had no financial education, they didn't seek knowledge and, worst of all, they remained in the mindset (mental pattern) of scarcity, poverty and difficulty. When wealth arrived, these people did everything they could (unconsciously) to return to the familiar pattern of scarcity, and they lost all their fortune, because they didn't change their thoughts, feelings and, consequently, their vibrations, which are what really connect us to good things!

Wanting to solve things "by magic", with games, is betting something and keeping expectations low.

Thousands of people are hoping to win.

However, you can make this money in another way. Here, I can tell you that the universe expects more from you than that: use your mission, your talent, your gifts to be rich and really BE rich.

Money alone doesn't make you rich.

But I'm not here to discourage you from winning at any game. In other words, I want to tell you: you are much more than that.

> "My ideas, energy and passion are creating wealth now.
>
> Abundance comes to me in various ways.
>
> Today is full of opportunities and I will take advantage of them."

12 I have a legal case and I used the Law of Attraction, but I couldn't win. What did I do wrong?

We always have to remember whether our goals are really tangible. We also have to know if they are correct.

What do I mean by that: are there any real chances of you winning this case? Is it too time-consuming, according to the lawyers or the justice system in your country?

Seeing all the details and even though it's a tangible goal, what you've done is right (determine all the goals that depend on you).

From that moment on, what you can do is vibrate at high frequencies of deservingness, joy at the process being resolved, and make visualizations of this process already being completed. Bring the feeling of justice, joy and deservingness to this visualization, feel it and, automatically, your vibration rises to connect with the solution to this case.

Change the axis. Instead of feeling bad, feel good and fulfilled. The Law of Attraction is not a top hat from which a rabbit will emerge, nor is it a magic wand. It's reality!

What's more, your process has another stakeholder, and these people are also vibrating. Keep going and believing, with the best feelings that can spring up inside you. Anger, hatred, resentment, haste, anxiety... None of this will help you at this time.

> "I deserve all the prosperity, justice and joy that money will bring me.
>
> Money is my natural right."

13 For the Law of Attraction to work, do you have to ask, feel and let go?

When they say to "let go", it's to let go of anxiety and worry about the goal.

The right thing to do is to always vibrate in what you want and keep it in mind, "letting go" of the anxiety about achieving your goal. This is another of the "bullshit" stories about the **Law of Attraction**, and it's very dangerous!

When we talk about "letting go", we think of sitting on the sofa and waiting for desire to manifest itself. BUT THAT'S NOT IT AT ALL! For the Law of Attraction to work properly and more quickly in your life, you need ACTION!

Without moving, nothing will happen. Or, what will happen, will be anything, because when we don't know where to go, any path will do. And that's not what we want! This book is about letting you know that your reality is in YOUR HANDS. But for that, you have to act! Without action, nothing happens. So when we talk about "letting go", it's about removing anxiety and sometimes even a certain obsession about desire.

When we vibrate in anxiety and obsession, we are vibrating at very low frequencies, which will connect us to situations of low value to us! To give you an idea, each emotion produces a measured vibration.

Take a look at this spiral I've prepared for you, based on the studies of Dr. David Hawkins, MD, PhD who was an internationally renowned psychiatrist, physician, researcher, spiritual teacher and author.

Emotions scale

700+	Lighting
600	Peace
540	Happiness
500	Love
400	Reason
350	Acceptance
310	Good will
250	Neutrality
200	Courage
175	Pride
150	Anger
125	Desire
100	Fear
75	Sadness
50	Apathy
30	Guilt
20	Shame

Dr. David Hawkins also said:

"Everything we do from the space of inner wisdom is certain before it even happens.

When we're on the right track, we have that internal certainty, and the result is already obvious to us."

Being obvious doesn't mean standing on top, disturbing and vibrating with feelings of mistrust.

Suspicion can be the famous "will it work out?" or "God willing…".

If you are sure of what you want and the realization of it is an absolute truth for you, the whole universe will move to make it happen.

You and the universe are one.

Remember!

"I choose to vibrate in love, joy and abundance, because then I know I can achieve my goals.

I let go of anxiety and embrace confidence and my ability to achieve more in my life."

14 Can I use the Law of Attraction to attract a specific person?

I think it's better for you to work on your inner self, on your development, on getting better and better, on increasing your vibration, so that you collapse with someone who vibrates in the same way as you.

The **Law of Attraction** works on an individual basis. You shouldn't interfere with someone else's path based solely on your own will.

"I love myself as I am **and I get better every day.**

That way, good people like me connect with me."

15 How do I change my energy signature?

First, let me explain what an energy signature is!

All our thoughts generate electromagnetic waves, which alter our feelings. Imagine a rainy day when you start thinking about that relationship that didn't work out. Automatically, you start to feel sad, guilty, homesick and alone.

That's it! Your thought has changed your feeling, which also emits electromagnetic waves, altering the vibration around you, which we call your energy signature.

You may have heard the expression before:

> "My saint didn't match up with that person **or** I don't like their energy, it's heavy!"

That's the energy signature!

It's what we vibrate! It's the energy around you, which I like to call your signature. It's like our signature when we write on a document. People know it's you because they recognize it.

We can have the energetic signature of the protagonist in life, the brave, the intelligent, the wise, the prosperous, or we can have the energetic signature of the victim, the complainer, the person who is always in failure and pain!

We change our energetic signature every time we pay attention to our thoughts.

Every thought passes through a "belief filter". It therefore makes sense to analyze the quality of your thoughts in relation to your emotional, financial and personal life.

Believing in difficulty will only bring more difficulty into our lives.

Remember: thoughts generate emotions which automatically trigger our vibration, thus producing our energetic signature.

If you want to change your signature, change the quality of your thoughts!

"**I'm incredibly** successful at everything.

I am strong and I have the power to create things that will allow me to live a more abundant life.

I'm sure of what I want.

I'm aware of what I want.

I'm aware of who I am."

16 Why doesn't the Law of Attraction work for me?

Often, we put our focus, our attention on something, but our feelings – the really deep ones – are connected to other situations.

What rules the Law of Attraction is not thought, but feeling.

In what you thought was impossible to happen, your feeling must have been so strong that it connected with your goal.

Our greatest difficulty is to understand our feelings, because our rational side interferes and directs us elsewhere, making us doubt what we feel.

Don't forget: it's the feeling that will activate the Law of Attraction for you!

Guilt is one of the feelings that blocks the Law of Attraction, preventing it from working quickly for you.

Guilt is living in the past. And there, nothing can be changed.

Leave whatever it is in its rightful place: in the past. Live for today!

As you focus on this thought, the more nourished it becomes. And that's not the point.

Focus forward.

The feeling of being undeserving is also one of the causes of the Law of Attraction being blocked.

What's the point of thinking you don't deserve your goal?

There will always be "excuses" external to you to justify your feeling of not deserving it

It's such a low-vibration feeling that you constantly feed it, and that's what you'll have in your reality.

Prosperity and abundance are the right of EVERYONE.

There are no chosen ones. There's no such thing as "this one or that one will do well, and that other one was born to do badly". This is a limiting belief and may be preventing you from achieving your goals, simply because your dominant thinking is still on scarcity.

"I create new thoughts, and so does the world around me.

I'm grateful for every positive change I see.

I'm ready to be healed.

I'm willing to forgive.

I'm willing to get rid of any feeling that doesn't make me move forward."

17 I don't believe in the Law of Attraction. How can I change that?

It doesn't matter whether you believe in the Law of Attraction or not. It's working all the time, whether or not you realize it or agree with it.

I feel this question is more of a defense of you. After all, if this were really your belief, you wouldn't even be here.

What frustration made you think that?

It is a universal law that we humans cannot change. It governs the planet and has already been discovered in depth by quantum physics, by great masters and scholars. Our molecules vibrate with our feelings and this has been scientifically proven.

The Law of Attraction allows you to connect with everything you want through the power of the mind, because thoughts are things: the house you want, the car or even the relationship you dream of, all pass through your thoughts, creating your reality.

Knowledge is a banquet that we serve, but we don't force anyone to eat.

The Law of Attraction is there for everyone, but it can't connect you to good things if you don't know its mechanism, its gears.

"I am now free of all the old resistance that no longer serves me.

I open my mind to the new and thus allow new creative ideas to come to me."

18 "Thoughts are things." What do you mean, William? I didn't understand that!

Everything that comes from our thoughts becomes something.

A chair we sit on, for example, was once just an idea in someone's head. All our external reality is no different from our internal reality.

When we see someone in trouble in life, we may wonder what they did to deserve it. But often, this person in difficulty has had a past in which they were not so nice, correct or fair, and there is a law that runs parallel to the Law of Attraction, which is the Law of Action and Reaction. This person may have done a lot of harm to someone or even cursed them, and so they can't co-create good things in their life.

Don't compare yourself when co-creating your reality. Comparison only hinders you.

Remember that thoughts are things, and whatever you think, you are creating.

The law responds to your thoughts, whatever they may be.

If you notice a car that you really like and find beautiful, you suddenly start seeing it all the time in traffic. If you hate someone, vibe on them and think about them, you meet them in the elevator.

You think about your ex-boyfriend so much that you run into him on the escalator at the mall.

I ask you: what were the odds?

Thoughts are things.

Believe in it and pay attention to the details.

Hold on to thoughts of what you want.

Make it perfectly clear.

You attract, you become, you live exactly what you think about most.

"I have the power, confidence and ability to achieve all my goals.

It's not for nothing that I've come this far, and I know I'll go further.

Trust lives in me, it is always welcome and accepted!"

19 Can you lose weight with the Law of Attraction?

What makes you lose weight is a regime, a diet, a healthier life, discipline and new attitudes. But the Law of Attraction does give you a boost!

We can use the Law of Attraction for any goal that is measurable, i.e. realistically achievable.

It's no use, for example, wanting to use the Law of Attraction to lose weight without taking care of your eating habits and eating excessively.

Your positive action is fundamental for the Law of Attraction to work correctly in your life. It's not enough just to have the goal and wait for it to magically resolve itself!

Law of Attraction is ACTION!

Think about it: you are a human transmission antenna. It sounds strange, but it's one of the greatest truths.

Your transmissions create your life and the world around you.

I say it's the most powerful antenna, because it goes beyond any city or country.

It has no borders and no limits. Human beings created all this. Look at nature: it has no fence. So your frequency goes out into the world through your thoughts!

You can attract a personal trainer who wants to help you, you can find a friend who has graduated in nutrition and now wants to do a new project and who will help you lose weight by giving you a balanced diet as a gift!

You'll see signs appear right in front of you if you take off your blindfold to look.

But it all started when you made a DECISION, and it was so strong that the whole universe then moved to help you.

If you want to change anything in your life, change the channel and change the frequency, changing your thoughts, enriching your life and helping the world to evolve with your victories.

Objective
measurable

Your goal needs to be tangible. You can't want to lose 10 kilos in a week, in a healthy way, after a lifetime of poor eating habits and no exercise. What would your achievable and healthy goal be?

Small daily goals

What are the small daily goals you can make towards your main objective? List things that you will actually do, so that you don't feel frustrated at the end of the day. The Law of Attraction harmonizes with your vibration. Promise what you will actually accomplish. It could be a small goal, like taking a walk around the block, for example.

"**From now on,** I make better food choices.

I like the foods that are best for my body **and I enjoy eating them.**

I love every cell in my body **and support its regeneration.**

I want to live healthier and healthier.

That's why I take loving care of my body."

20 How can blocking feelings influence the Law of Attraction in someone's life?

There are feelings in our unconscious, preventing the Law of Attraction from working quickly in our lives and, if we don't realize this, we can cause the Law of Attraction to become too slow, too sluggish or too heavy and life doesn't move forward.

For example, you really want to go on an international trip and you work hard. Then obstacles start to happen: the passport doesn't come through, your vacation days have been changed or whatever. But you could have created this travel reality in 3 months! However, with the feelings in your unconscious stuck, it takes you much longer. Sometimes it can even take years to achieve the goal that could easily be achieved if there were no blockages.

You are vibrating in these feelings, they will connect to your reality, and more blockages will appear in your life.

In question 13, I explain more about the Scale of Emotions. If you haven't seen it yet, it's worth studying this question too.

To give you an idea, feelings are so strong that they emit a vibration that can be measured in hertz.

A feeling of fear, for example, emits a vibration of 100 hertz.

This totally blocks any rapid co-creation.

If you were to take that international trip now, it would take about two years to happen, because when you vibrate in fear, the results are more fear. The universe brings you more of the same.

What result do you get from feeling afraid?

More situations of fear, dread and insecurity. This generates an avalanche of toxic feelings for dreams.

"I accept change and can easily adjust to new situations.

I always learn new things when I trust myself and know that the best is yet to come!"

21 How long does it take to see the results of the Law of Attraction?

I could answer you with another question: why don't most people live the life of their dreams?

That's the problem! The vast majority of people think about what they don't want and, without knowing it, they're creating more of that reality, because that's exactly what they emit.

When you ask me how long it takes to see results, you're dissociating yourself from the law. You're putting yourself side by side and not inside. The whole thing is inside your head.

If you emit an electromagnetic wave of abundance, you will spend your day seeing business opportunities, new learning, people coming to you with profitable ideas.

This can also take a week, a month or a year. But from the moment you study and learn how the Law of Attraction works, you have already changed your frequency.

A marathon runner trains for a year to win a race by a thousandth of a second. You've spent 30 years thinking negatively and you want the Law of Attraction to give you signs right now, today, as if it owed it to you!

It's as if you were saying, in other words: "Either I see the signs or I don't believe in all this Law of Attraction stuff!". That's what you're saying with your question.

The Law of Attraction works at an accelerated rate in your life, but if you stick to the same thought pattern, your results will be the same.

Remember: you are where you are and, as we seek knowledge, we leave the place where we already know what's going on and move into a new reality in which we can co-create anything and command our reality as the protagonist of our story.

I often make a nice analogy: when we go on a long trip, we can take the bus and spend a few hours, or buy a plane ticket and arrive at our destination in minutes.

Knowing about the Law of Attraction is your ticket to your dreams!

"**I am now free of** all the old resistance **that no longer serves me.**

I open my mind to the new **and thus allow** new profitable ideas to come to me."

22. You say that our thoughts become feelings and vibrations. Is that the Law of Attraction?

That's not all there is to the Law of Attraction.

What you asked me is part of the process.

If that were all there was to it, it would be very simple. That's just one stage. It's a gear that flows all the time and, when we understand it, that's when we accelerate the Law of Attraction.

When we talk about thought, feeling and vibration, we're talking about a part of quantum physics that has helped to understand the Law of Attraction, which for many years was seen only as a process of "visualization" and "letting go".

We're not brought up to think positively, much less to have faith, to believe.

This is the biggest obstacle of the century.

We grew up being taught to use "I don't want to".

- I don't want to be forgotten.
- I don't want to be mugged.
- I don't want to be betrayed.
- I don't want to get sick.
- I don't want to be single.

You now have the necessary knowledge. You know that you can change this frequency by saying:

- I'm confident!
- It's safe here!
- I trust myself!
- I'm healthy!
- I want to get married!

These are just examples of moments when the mind is working forwards and not backwards.

If you say "my memory isn't good, my memory is bad", you're training your head backwards.

Use: "my memory is getting better and better, my memory has improved a lot over the years".

What's the most negative phrase you use in your day?

_____

_____

_____

_____

What would it be like now in a positive way, pulling you forward? After writing it down, repeat it out loud and feel the difference!

_____

_____

_____

_____

"I'm always in touch with my creative source.

My creative source is always in touch with me."

23 How does it work when we think of something and the exact opposite happens?

I'll say it again: it's your dominant thinking that generates everything.

The **Law of Attraction** is a law of nature.

It's impersonal and doesn't differentiate between good and bad things.

It perceives your vibration, harmonizes with it and reflects it back to you in the form of life experience.

We think one thing, but the unconscious – which is where our most powerful and true thoughts germinate – is vibrating differently.

For example, we can spend all our time thinking positively about something and, when it happens, it's not what we expected. This happens because, unconsciously, we vibrate in fear or worry, which is much stronger than positive thinking.

It will always be the FEELING that will determine the positive or negative collapse in your vibration!

The Law of Attraction is a secondary law and is parallel to the Law of Vibration, which is the primary law and which is affected by our feelings. So it's fear and worry that will bring tone to your reality, not your rational expectation, your rationally created desire.

"**I have** the right keys for the right locks. I can open any door **I want.**

The key to happiness is knowing that my thoughts create my experiences.

I use this key in all areas of my life.

I love myself **and everything is fine!**"

24 How do we find out which blockages are getting in our way?

The Law of Attraction is very obedient every time.

When you align yourself with the things you want and focus on them, then everything happens.

When we want something very much and realize that we can't access it, we must have a blockage and often we don't know which is the main "column" holding up a building. Removing one of these "columns" can be dangerous, because we don't know which one is supporting the whole structure. So we can't determine just one "column", such as fear.

We can't say that fear alone blocks a person. It could be a trauma from someone or some situation. That's why it's so important to always analyze what lies behind the apparent, to delve into the layers. This path of understanding blockages is a long road, along which we walk with a rucksack full of stones on our back and, as we deepen our emotional knowledge, we take one stone at a time out of that rucksack of life and, in this way, it begins to be seen in a different light.

Our unconscious mind is like a garden. It's our conscious mind that sows the seeds and we often forget that we planted them. But in our unconscious, it continues to germinate.

Watch what you're planting, reader!

"I reinterpret life without judgment.

I look inside and connect with the part of me that knows how to heal.

I breathe in the breath of life, which nourishes and regenerates me.

I invite you to remove any frequency that is negative.

I pay loving attention and take care of myself like never before.

I know that all my feelings are my partners and want my best."

25 Is discouragement a block to the Law of Attraction?

Discouragement is a self-sabotage that makes you procrastinate. Because it doesn't appear overnight, it grows inside you and becomes a habit.

We need to break this negative cycle.

Discouraged, the Law of Attraction slows down your co-creations.

Think: if you're slow, why would the universe be speeding up? Remember that everything has its time, including you.

If the discouragement lasts just one day, that's normal. We all have a day like that. It's not normal to be overwhelmed and discouraged forever.

Our body often wants to stay in its comfort zone so that we don't have to work, because by staying in that zone we don't expend any energy. Discouragement can therefore be self-sabotage, blocking the mind from changing so that we remain in the same safe place.

There's no doubt that discouragement hinders the Law of Attraction from working more quickly, but it's interesting to think about where discouragement comes from. A lack of dreams? A lack of belief in yourself? From poor self-esteem? Limiting beliefs that have been installed in your mind?

Look deeply into where this discouragement comes from, because it is only the representation of some feeling that is not so healthy.

To thrive, you have to change!

I'll help you with 5 new habits!

Always start with the first step and work your way up. You'll feel the change over the next few days.

Here are some tips for getting rid of discouragement and living a happier, more energetic life!

Before long, you'll have new habits and the Law of Attraction, which harmonizes with your vibration, will start flowing positively again.

Who does it all depend on? On you!

5 new habits
that will save you from discouragement!

1. Make short, medium and long-term plans.

Have well-established plans that you will stick to (so as not to get frustrated later). Keep your feet on the ground.

2. Try to eat properly and sleep well.

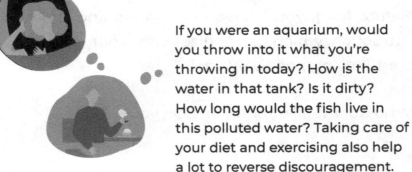

If you were an aquarium, would you throw into it what you're throwing in today? How is the water in that tank? Is it dirty? How long would the fish live in this polluted water? Taking care of your diet and exercising also help a lot to reverse discouragement.

3. Give yourself presents from time to time.

Appreciate every step or goal you achieve. The brain loves rewards. You're training it, just like we train animals. And there's nothing wrong with that.

4. Get rid of toxic relationships, heavy, complaining and negative people.

Try to talk to people who add things, people who dream, talk about prosperity and are cheerful.

5. Against discouragement, invest in self-knowledge.

Occupy your mind with wisdom, as you are doing now with this book. But never stop! This is a lifelong habit.

"My life is always new and this is a new day.

It's a pleasure and a joy to plant new seeds, because I know that they will become my new good stages.

My whole life is conducive to good things!

I trust in this process and am grateful for every step! Gratitude!"

26 Can I use the Law of Attraction to win the lottery?

I've already talked about this a bit in question 11, but let's take a deeper look.

Pay attention, I'm going to make an analogy with a parking space for your car, to make it easier to understand: when you go to park your car, you keep thinking about the space you want to use, but, just like you, many people are also thinking about a space. What's more, there's the parking lot owner nearby, who also wants you to stop there and pay.

Can you see where I'm going with this?

The flow of the Law of Attraction is great for bringing a lot of things into your life, but if you focus only on winning the lottery, as if that were going to solve absolutely all your problems, the Law of Attraction can say: "Fine, I can even help you win, but what will become of your life after that?"

Understand: it's not just about winning, having the prize. In fact, if you research lottery winners, you'll see that many have become poor again, or even poorer than they were before.

Often, winning the lottery may not be the solution.

What I'm about to tell you may be very controversial, but all the money on the planet already exists. How to bring it to you is the big question. And you don't have to win the lottery, you can use the Law of Attraction to bring you all the money you want.

Imagine how many millionaires there are out there who didn't win the lottery, who made their own money.

If you follow me on social media, you'll know that I always tell you about my own life experience, about going from being a market trader to becoming the family's first millionaire.

At this very moment, there is more money being made in the world, and it is going into the hands of people like you and me. Bringing in this money can be done in various ways: using your creativity, your intelligence, your gift, your talent to create an idea. And then you make your money instead of earning it.

When people make money and aren't prosperous, they end up losing the money that came in.

You can work on your thinking to be a creative person who will work to bring that money to you, and the Law of Attraction will help you with that.

> "I meet incredible people who will have a positive influence on my finances.
>
> I know there's more money being made for me right now and it will find its way to me."

27 When the fear is so great that you can't co-create anything... What do you do?

Fear and faith are two things that you need to believe in and that you don't see.

For example, if you're afraid of a bug or insect, even if you can't see it, you're vibrating in fear. As human magnets, we think, feel, vibrate and attract. In this way, you make the bug come to you!

You've connected this fear to you!

The same goes for people who are afraid of mugging and are always mugged, people who are afraid of losing their money and always lose it, people who are afraid of being betrayed and always are. They are attracting that into their reality.

When you're afraid of running out of money, for example, that's the message you're sending to the universe: you're out of money!

When you vibrate in scarcity, you create more scarcity, because the universe always gives us more of the same. So, if we vibrate in fear, there will be more situations that make us feel that fear.

Fear is so selfish that it wants everything for itself. So it creates fearful situations all the time!

Don't focus on fear, focus on

FAITH - SPIRITUAL STRENGTH.

Your spiritual strength!

Ask yourself questions like:

1. Is it my fear?

2. Why do I think that?

3. Who do I know who is always afraid?

4. What bad situations have happened to make me afraid?

Fear only has room if you let it.

Don't germinate negative thoughts.

Focus on the good things that have happened to you today.

They can be as simple as: "I got a paçoquinha today," or "My coworker served me such delicious coffee!".

You send positive orders to your mind and things flow.

"My mind is totally creative.

Ideas come to me easily and without any effort.

I enjoy new things and learn from them."

28 When you say that the Law of Attraction can be accelerated, does that mean that this acceleration is natural, as long as I change my vibration pattern?

When you have the Law of Attraction blocked, things don't arrive and when you align yourself with the gears of the Law of Attraction, you naturally accelerate your results.

Now imagine a tap that, when you turn it on, very little water comes out - where a lot of water should be coming out. Then we clean the pipe that was disturbing the flow of water and, when we open the tap again, the water flows in abundance.

The pipe has been unclogged, unblocked. And with the Law of Attraction, it's the same: it's natural for it to flow in abundance, it's us who don't understand it and use it in the wrong way.

"I'm a happy and good expression of life.

Everything comes to me with ease, joy and glory."

29 Does being a "cowhand" affect the Law of Attraction in my life?

The Law of Attraction is about flow, prosperity and abundance and when you, at all times, choose the worst for you, the cheapest, you send the universe the message that you accept the worst and so the worst can come to you, yes!

You, being a "cowhand", are sending out a message of lack, of scarcity, all the time.

The stingy person says all the time that they're in want!

She may have the money, but she doesn't use it, it doesn't flow.

The energy that this person is sending out into the universe all the time is that of lack.

Over the years, I've met people in my office, when I was a therapist, who would lock up food so others wouldn't eat it, collect pieces of soap to make a new one, always go to the market to get the cheapest and worst things, etc.

What kind of message is this person sending out to the universe? What kind of wave is your cosmic antenna sending out at this moment?

These are important questions for me to ask you.

No one is telling you to buy the most expensive things to show off, or to do crazy things when you can't afford them, but when you can afford them and don't do them, it does drastically disrupt your life.

The flow of money, of prosperity, is mentally acting in your life because you think, feel and vibrate, and so you create an energetic signature around you that connects you to all the things we have.

A stingy person is a person who doesn't flow, doesn't evolve and only brings more situations to reinforce this reality in their life!

"I always find ways to attract more and more money and there's nothing wrong with that!

Prosperity is my ally and I feel good about it."

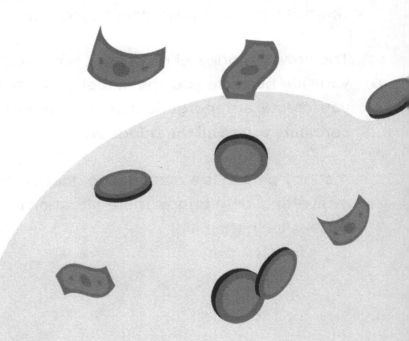

30 Can we change our unconscious to attract better things faster?

Yes. But wait, because I have to explain this to you: the mind is divided into the conscious and the unconscious. The conscious is where we are attentive, paying attention.

When we consciously work on positive thoughts and have attitudes of prosperity and abundance, we are reprogramming our unconscious, especially when we feel rejection, guilt or unworthiness - which can be in your unconscious without you realizing it, thus attracting poverty into your life.

If we worry about money, we are working our unconscious towards scarcity, towards lack, and more lack we bring upon ourselves.

We need to reprogram our minds for profitable, creative ideas and ways to build a new direction in our lives. Understand that you're not going to erase everything that's in your unconscious black box, but rather send it new information, little by little, using your conscious mind as a gateway.

I can say that the conscious mind is the airplane and the unconscious mind is the black box, recording everything that happens in the aircraft.

> "I live in the present and choose to have more money in the present.
>
> I trust in my power of manifestation and that's why so many good things happen to me."

31 Can I attract things to other people using the Law of Attraction?

The Law of Attraction respects free will. So, if you want to attract things to your child, for example, you have to know if that's what they want.

Many people think that their happiness is also the other person's happiness, but in this case it is the person's free will that prevails, because universal laws respect the will of each person.

The Law of Attraction works on respect, before anything else. My tip is: use the Law of Attraction for yourself and, every time you want to attract something to someone, think of them as happy, healthy, creative and with all the skills they possess.

The "script" that's in your head isn't always the script of happiness for the other person, okay?

"**Today, I can see that** the other person is acting the way they can be.

I am who I am and I allow him to be who he is.

Silence, respecting each other's time."

32 How can we control thoughts that automatically come into our minds?

This is one of the biggest questions I get from people.

Every time thoughts come into our minds, especially negative ones, I do an exercise that I'm going to teach you now: when the bad thought comes, I ask myself: "Is this my thought?". Then you bring out your truth: "I wouldn't think that!".

We don't control our thoughts, we just deal with them. Thoughts come and go, and we pick up the field we're in. Sometimes the thought isn't even yours, it's just in the extrasensory field that you've picked up from another person or place.

When a bad thought comes along, immediately replace it with a better one.

It works! We are the only beings who can "think about our thoughts" and it's a real blessing that we can control them!

"I have the sensitivity to make good choices.

I respect my inner voice, I talk to it and we always come to good decisions."

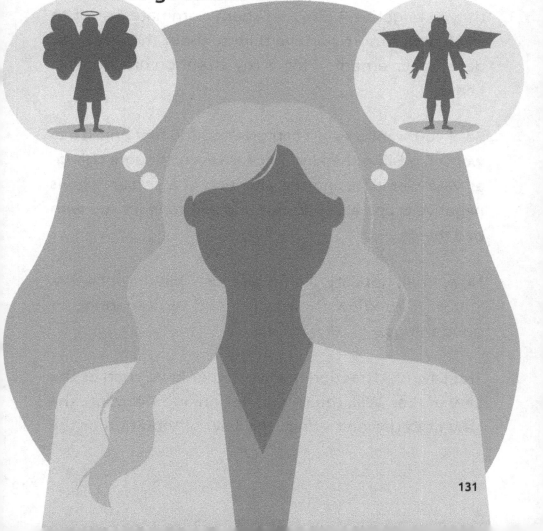

33. Is there a step-by-step process for applying the Law of Attraction in my daily life, or is it a study that takes effect over time?

The Law of Attraction is a cog in the wheel, but there are steps you can start taking right now. The law just is, it's natural. However, the more you study it, the more aware you become of this process. I, for example, pay attention to the thoughts that come into my mind. If they're negative, I don't let them dominate. I start to think about more positive things, about the week's or day's achievements, I focus my attention on the tasks I have.

So, if you want a step, I can give you the first one: it's to work on positive thinking. Because every thought changes your vibration, and the vibration of a person who is negative is bad and harmful, and will connect you with bad things.

Now, in all honesty, it's no use just thinking positive. You have to know the process and BE a magnet for good things.

The Law of Attraction involves other laws, such as the Law of Free Will, the Law of Action and Reaction, the Law of Cause and Effect, the Law of Vibration or the

Law of Reciprocity. Therefore, study is necessary to achieve the most efficient results.

"My thoughts are the stepping stones to my success, because I learn from them.

With every step I climb, I get stronger.

I've learned that I don't need to see the whole ladder, I celebrate and trust myself with each step. That's how I climb higher and higher."

34 They say you can use the Law of Attraction to make someone else think of you. Is this true?

You've probably experienced something like this: you've been thinking a lot about someone and they send you a message, or you've been wanting to talk to them and they call you or show up.

What you activated at that moment was not just the Law of Attraction. You activated the power of your mind, which emanates a vibration.

The mind is energy, and that energy goes wherever you want it to. But we must always bear in mind that we mustn't hurt anyone's free will or free choice!

We can't force people to think about us, and here's a thought: do you really want to manipulate the other person's thinking?

Is that really accurate?

Wouldn't it be nicer if the person thought of you of their own free will?

"My focus is me.

I make my happiness my biggest goal!

I give myself the best, I put myself in the best and I only accept the best."

35

When we're vibrating in something good and suddenly negative thoughts come up that we've been carrying around all our lives and that "erase" that good vibration that was there before, is there any way to get me back to the good vibration?

It doesn't "erase" the good vibe you were in. You've simply changed the vibe.

It's like a radio where you're listening to rock music, and you press the button and tune in to another radio station. Then, by changing the station, you change the frequency.

When we think, we are in a vibrational frequency and when we change that thought, we also change our vibrational frequency.

If you want to vibrate positively, you have to change your thoughts. You have that power. If you were thinking positive and changed to negative, then the opposite is also true.

The choice is yours alone to let bad thoughts invade what is good!

"My positive and good mind **attracts positive experiences for me.**"

36 How can I vibrate that I deserve a job if I've been unemployed for months?

When we're unemployed, it's often the worst time of our lives, when we can feel useless and our vibration drops a lot. In this case, it means that you've been in the same fragile vibration for months.

There are many jobs available on the market and you are available too.

A job has an energy and a vibration that you need to connect with. But it's not just about sending in a CV. You're going to be different from all the other CVs: you're going to FOCUS on the company you want to work for, and then research the people who work in that company.

You'll see if you have the profile, the requirements. You'll do a lot of research focused on the company you want. You don't want to go "shooting" all over the place, without being clear about what you want. This way, you'll be focused and your chances will be much better.

This research will get you excited about the solution and the job you want.

Tip!

Sometimes you're looking for a job, but have you ever thought that you could be an entrepreneur and offer jobs to other people? Those who always hit the same key always hear the same sound.

The Law of Attraction says that your thoughts change your vibration, which in turn connects you to everything you want most.

If you want a job, prepare yourself. Study to connect to the job, and it will connect to you!

There's no point in thinking about a job if you don't prepare for it, because there are other people who are preparing for it, and they will pass you by.

ACTION is extremely important for working on your vibration.

"The perfect job is looking for me **and it's** getting closer and closer."

37

William, I'm on disability pension and have a chronic illness. I need a job that won't jeopardize my pension. I have a master's degree in literature and a lot of studies.

In your own question you've already given me all your context, your panorama, a map, but without knowing where you're going with it.

You've said it all, but at the same time you've said nothing.

None of that matters, because you haven't said what you want!

Do you want a job?
Opening a business?
Cure yourself?
What's this job like?
Where is it?
How long do you want this job?
Is it measurable?

When we "grope" this map, everything becomes clearer, so that we know where we want to go. You have to get out of complaining and into clarity and focus. Otherwise, any path may be valid for you.

"I don't complain anymore, my heart is filled with gratitude.

I like to say thank you **and that's how things flow.**

I see myself in success **and I know he sees me too."**

38. When I stop feeling rejected by a certain situation, does that mean my mind has unblocked?

Your mind wasn't blocked because you felt rejection. Rejection is just a feeling that's inside you and, when you feel it, you push away a series of opportunities. Because those who usually suffer from rejection either reject or think they're being rejected all the time. And then, when you let go of this feeling, you have a release, not an unblocking and, without a doubt, everything starts to flow better in your life.

"**I love and** approve of myself as I am.

I accept myself completely **and I'm very happy to always give my best.**"

39

How do I deal with the feeling of always being "sucked in" by someone negative around me? How do I keep my energy up?

Your question is interesting, and the name of it is vampirism.

There are many books and studies about this. I decided to answer this question for one reason only: to tell you that only those who can be sucked in are sucked in.

You allow it to happen. Do you know how? By giving an audience to these things, by giving attention to these people. Where is your focus? Where is your energy?

When you say that your energy is being sucked away, you're opening the door for this to happen. If I'm in an environment with negative people, I simply ignore their vibration. The evil in the world only has room in the evil in me!

If you allow this, it's because you've lowered your frequency to match the frequency of the person who wants to suck you in, and you're serving them up as a feast! Stick to high-vibration feelings, such as love, joy, enthusiasm and creativity, so that you don't collapse with this vampire by your side!

"I respect the energy of that person (you can speak their name) and I'm grateful for what I've learned.

Now I want to disconnect from her energetic vibration.

I love myself and everything is fine!"

40 How do I know if I'm practicing the Law of Attraction correctly?

The Law of Attraction is governing you, you're just not practicing it. This is just an expression to make it easier for you to learn. Right now, I know it's working properly for me when I start getting small results.

To do this, you need to be awake, you need to have full attention in your life.

You don't have to start visualizing a big goal - for example, a car, which could take a few months. You can envision small goals before something big. Build up security, certainty and confidence. These are things that need to grow in you.

Don't be in doubt!

Doubt is linked to lack, and it always weakens us! Trust yourself more and forget that "they're sucking you dry" thing. You're not a cup and you're not a straw!

Be the best you can be!

"The universe is responding **to all my intentions!**

My wishes **are coming true fast!**

I recognize every little victory **I have!"**

41 Does the Law of Attraction interfere with our destiny?

I don't believe in fate, I don't believe in pre-established things.

I use and practice in my life the Law of Free Choice, commonly known as "free will". So, I build my future through the choices I make now, through effort, studies, actions, decisions...

"**I recognize in myself** all the power of the universe.

Everything comes to me with ease, joy and glory.

All the potential for love and abundance **flows through me.**"

42

My husband is extremely negative and that saddens me because I love him. How do I deal with this situation?

You are not him! Understand that.

It's his way, and there will come a time in his life when he wakes up. What he can't do is interfere with your positivity. Because sometimes you're excited about a certain project and the "negative husband" starts to destroy all your enthusiasm, and it's very difficult to live with someone like that in your home. However, we can't block ourselves with this!

Your husband will start to be positive the moment he sees your results.

And if he doesn't understand, that's fine too. Each soul has its own time.

There are awake people and there are asleep people.

It's not your husband's small-mindedness that will make you block yourself.

You love him just the way he is, but you have to follow your dreams. Remember that every soul is unique. You are eternal with yourself, and it's up to you to work on your prosperity and show your results to the "negative husband".

Focus on your evolution and your awakening and, naturally, your husband will begin to change too.

Accept it and never try to change it. Simply SHOW him your results and he'll draw his own conclusions!

Now, if he forbids you to study, imprisons you, puts you down, humiliates you etc., these are other issues.

It's called a toxic relationship, and it's up to you to decide whether you want to stay in it or not.

Life is made up of choices.

"I feel safe and fulfilled in everything I do and how I do it.

I deny what you deny me and move on in peace."

43 Is it wrong to co-create the "dream house" instead of co-create the renovation of the current house?

No. If you like the house you have and want to renovate it, it's a desire. Napoleon Hill talks a lot about "burning desire". That's what you need to determine. What is your burning desire?

If you're in a house and want a new one, that's another wish.

They are different desires. What you need to do is choose one of them and focus.

This co-creation is not wrong. You're working on the judgment that puts us in a situation of scarcity and conformity, limiting our growth and evolution.

If it's a new house, there's no problem. I've moved about eight times myself. Do you know what I do? I thank the house that took me in, sheltered me, served me, and I go on my way. Nothing is fixed. Everything is made up of cycles that end for others to begin. The house I left will be the new house for someone who will arrive.

Our soul naturally likes what is beautiful and good. So I leave you with a question: why limit the limitless?

> "I reinterpret life without judgment.
>
> I look inside and connect with the part of me that knows how to be prosperous.
>
> I connect with all the abundance that exists in the universe."

44 Does the Law of Attraction have to do with religion?

No, the Law of Attraction has nothing to do with religion, which means "reconnecting". It's how you connect to God. It can be through an evangelical church, umbanda, candomblé, spiritism, it doesn't matter.

The Law of Attraction is a natural universal law, like the Law of Polarity, the Law of Gravity and the Law of Cause and Effect, for example.

You can have the religion you want, with the label you want. That label we assume will often do us good. A religion makes sense if it does you good and makes you a better human being. So it doesn't matter what religion you have, what matters is how you think.

The Law of Attraction is a universal law that is governing you, whether you agree with it or not, because the Law of Attraction is not esotericism, the Law of Attraction is a universal law, which we study so that we can understand how it works and, when we learn the content better, we can apply it to our lives and have better results. In other words: it has nothing to do with religion, it's a SCIENCE!

"I'm always in touch with my creative source.

My creative source is always in touch with me."

45 Does the Law of Attraction need to be activated to work?

No.

It may be blocked, and it will work very slowly for you and for the things you want, but it is already working.

It's like thinking: "I don't believe the sea exists". But it is there and we know it.

It's the same with the Law of Attraction: you don't need to activate it, it's already active. Only when you understand the gears of the Law of Attraction, how it works, can you bring faster results and good results into your own life.

I can say out loud: "I don't believe in the sea!". But the wave comes and carries you away. We are a tiny speck in this immensity called the universe.

Learn to use the laws that govern you to flow better with everything you dream of.

It's already active and it's up to you to learn how to use it.

"I was born with all the skills and abilities within me, and I develop them more and more each day."

46 Is it possible to use the Law of Attraction to treat physical and emotional pain?

Both emotional and physical pain first appear in our thoughts.

So, you may not believe it, but in your unconscious there are blockages, fears, traumas and, over the years, you can create a reality of pain, depression, panic syndrome.

Some call this somatization.

It all starts with a thought, which can be a negative thought that germinates within your unconscious. Remember that the conscious is where we pay attention to everything. The problem is when we throw the seed into the unconscious and sometimes forget about it, but it's working inside us.

It's like walking, chewing, blinking.

We learn it once and our body does it without us even realizing it. It's the same with the Law of Attraction: it works involuntarily in our lives.

If you focus on your pain (a pain in your knee, for example), you're putting your thoughts and attention on the pain, and when you put your attention on something, the object of your attention expands, enlarges, increases. In other words, if you don't want to be in pain, depressed or anxious, don't focus on the pain. Focus on things that have been resolved, mentalize your knee healing, mentalize yourself going to physiotherapy. Don't visualize yourself in pain, visualize yourself in healing, because when you visualize, your mind already works its energy, and your body believes it.

It is possible to build a new emotional and physical reality for yourself using the Law of Attraction.

"My body is capable of regenerating itself **again and again.**

I feel good **every time I wake up or go to sleep.**

I rest my mind, and my body **rests in tranquility.**

Everything's fine!

I love myself **and everything is fine!"**

47 Is the Law of Attraction a form of prayer?

Praying is when we talk to God, meditating is when we fall silent to listen to God. They are two different things, but what do these two things have to do with the Law of Attraction?

The Law of Attraction is not a form of prayer and it is not a form of meditation.

The Law of Attraction is simply a universal law.

When you pray, you are talking, through your inner voice, to God, to your religiosity. Because when you pray, you begin to work words of love, words of hope, words of enthusiasm into your thoughts, and what often happens when you pray is that you pray the wrong way.

See the difference between these prayers:

"God, send rain where I live, because the animals are dying and I'm starving!"

Note that the way of praying is in lack, and is very different from praying like this:

"Thank you for my house, thank you for the rain that hasn't come yet, but I know it will. Thank you for this wind, thank you!"

Realize how different it is to be in scarcity, with words of lack flowing through your head, which end up bringing you even more lack.

The Law of Attraction is not a form of prayer, but the way you think within prayer can interfere with the co-creation of your reality!

"**My heart is the** center of my strength.

I listen attentively to each beat and line up in calm.

My mind and heart **go together!**

I trust my sixth sense and the universe.

I'm sensitive enough to understand all the messages from the universe."

48 Is there any method for the Law of Attraction to work faster?

Yes, there is a method called **Quintessence: accelerated Law of Attraction**.

It's a method to help people co-create a new reality more quickly.

In this method, five hidden feelings are revealed that, if they live inside your chest, you won't be able to accelerate the Law of Attraction.

It's working for everyone. What happens is that some people are asleep and don't understand this law, which is exactly why there's a lot of talk about spirituality and "awakening of consciousness", which is when we know a law, a rule, and awaken. But many people are still asleep and don't understand this law, which is so all-encompassing.

We talk a lot about co-creation.

God is creator and we are co-creators of our reality. It's the same when I write a book: I am the author and, if there is another author, they will be the co-author - or co-creator.

Let's imagine it like this: God was the author of this marvelous world we live in and we humans are co-creators, and we have a law parallel to the Law of Attraction, which is the Law of Free Will. So the Law of Attraction is a cog in the wheel, and you need to know the Law of Free Will, because your choices make your reality.

It all starts with faith, which is the assumption of believing in something invisible. However, there is another invisible thing, which is fear.

When people think about fear, they are emanating an energy of scarcity, lack, pain and depression, and when they work on faith, strength, will, hope and fulfillment, their paths open up. These are two invisible things, and it's very difficult to make human beings believe in something they can't see. Generally, we believe in what we can pick up, in the concrete. We doubt the invisible a lot, and we only start to believe when the results start to show.

"You are supreme intelligence, because you were created by intelligence itself.

You love yourself and everything is fine!

This is one of the best moments of your life!

Everything is working for your good, opening up your prosperity!

Never worry. What's yours will find a way to get to you."

49 My friend doesn't believe in the Law of Attraction, she thinks it's all nonsense. How can this influence me?

It only influences you if you tell her about your projects. Because your little friend "doesn't believe in the Law of Attraction" is her problem!

You're so open-minded, and you're worried about what your little friend is thinking?

I don't care what my little friend is thinking. I need to be with myself, I need to put myself first and I need to believe in my projects. When your little friend sees your results, she'll say: "Wow! And didn't it really work?". Then she'll ask you how you use the Law of Attraction, which until then she didn't even believe in.

If you let your friend's negative energy into your life, you won't be able to apply the Law of Attraction in an accelerated way. It will work so slowly that you'll come back to your friend and tell her that she was right, that the Law of Attraction doesn't really work.

"All my relationships are harmonious. I always think and express myself clearly and easily, so that the other person understands me better, and I them."

50 Now that I've studied everything about the Law of Attraction, can I stop studying and the Law will take care of everything?

No!

We never know everything.

At the moment I'm writing this book, I'm finishing my postgraduate degree in Neuroscience and Behavior at PUC-RS and entering a master's degree in Quantum Physics.

We must never stop studying.

A good doctor never stops studying, a good teacher never stops studying, a good lawyer never stops studying.

Why should we stop studying?

Every moment you learn something new, discover something new.

It's not just about thinking positive and that's it!

It's at this point that many people get frustrated, because they think that just by thinking positive, things will happen. And then, of course, they don't. Then they go off saying that they thought positively and did everything right, but that nothing happened.

The Law of Attraction is a gear, and you have to understand many things beyond the Law of Attraction itself.

When a person thinks positive thoughts and doesn't manage to bring things about, it's because they haven't understood the Law of Attraction as a system. First, a thought generates a feeling, which produces a vibration, and this vibration changes the molecules in your body. Quantum physics has been explaining exactly this, and we know that the attention of that observer, in front of that molecule, alters its life. So, when you're inside yourself and you make a thought - even if it's positive - if you don't visualize it and feel it, you won't be able to get the Law of Attraction to bring you the things you want in an easy way.

If you go back now and read any question at random, you'll discover new things that you couldn't see before.

Good studies!

They've only just begun!

> "I create new thoughts and the world around me changes too.
>
> I'm grateful for every positive change I receive.
>
> I'm ready for prosperity.
>
> I'm willing to be prosperous.
>
> I love myself and everything is fine!"

WILLIAM SANCHES

Follow me on social media

🌐 www.williamsanches.com

▶ williamsanchesvideos
Law of Attraction Channel No secrets

📷 @williamsanchesoficial

f /williamsanchesoficial